WORDS TO KNOW

lawns

museum

President

Washington, D.C.

White House

SIGHT WORDS

a
all
also
are
around
come
day
every
green
I
in
is
it
large
lives
many
people
see
the
there
to
where

I see the **White House**!

CHILD

The **White House** is a government building in the United States.

ADULT

I READ! YOU READ!

Child's Turn to Read

Adult's Turn to Read

WE READ ABOUT

THE WHITE HOUSE

Amy Culliford and Madison Parker

TABLE OF CONTENTS

SEAHORSE PUBLISHING

Parent and Caregiver Guide

Reading aloud with your child has many benefits. It expands vocabulary, sparks discussion, and promotes an emotional bond. Research shows that children who have books read aloud to them have improved language skills, leading to greater school success.

I Read! You Read! books offer a fun and easy way to read with your child. Follow these guidelines.

Before Reading

- Look at the front and back covers. Discuss personal experiences that relate to the topic.
- Read the *Words to Know* on page 3. Talk about what the words mean.
- If the book will be challenging or unfamiliar to your child, read it aloud by yourself the first time. Then, invite your child to participate in a second reading.

During Reading

CHILD Have your child read the words beside this symbol. This text has been carefully matched to the reading and grade levels shown on the cover.

ADULT You read the words beside this symbol.

- Stop often to discuss what you are reading and to make sure your child understands.
- If your child struggles with decoding a word, help them sound it out. If it is still a challenge, say the word for your child and have them repeat it after you.
- To find the meaning of a word, look for clues in the surrounding words and pictures.

After Reading

- Praise your child's efforts. Notice how they have grown as a reader.
- Ask and answer questions about the book.
- Discuss what your child learned and what they liked or didn't like about the book.

Most importantly, let your child know that reading is fun and worthwhile. Keep reading together as your child's skills and confidence grow.

White House

The White House is in **Washington, D.C.**

CHILD

Washington, D.C., is the capital of the United States.

ADULT

UNITED STATES OF AMERICA

Washington, D.C.

It is a **museum.** CHILD

A **museum** is a place where you can see important and historic items. ADULT

museum

It is also where the **President** lives.

CHILD

The **President** of the United States is elected every four years. The President leads the country.

ADULT

President
PRESIDENT OF THE UNITED

There are large green **lawns** all around it.

CHILD

The White House has a North **Lawn** and a South Lawn.

ADULT

lawns

Many people come to see the White House every day!

CHILD

On average, 6,000 people visit the White House grounds every day.

ADULT

ONE WAY
NO PARKING ANY TIME

Index

Written by: Amy Culliford and Madison Parker
Design by: Under the Oaks Media
Series Development: James Earley
Editor: Kim Thompson

Photos: Luca Perra: cover; Sagittarius Pro: p. 4-5; Chandler West: p. 9; archna nautiyal: p. 11; Wangkun Jia: p. 12-13; Lissandra Melo: p. 15

Library of Congress PCN Data
We Read About the White House / Amy Culliford and Madison Parker
I Read! You Read!
ISBN 979-8-8873-5189-6 (hard cover)
ISBN 979-8-8873-5209-1 (paperback)
ISBN 979-8-8873-5229-9 (EPUB)
ISBN 979-8-8873-5249-7 (eBook)
Library of Congress Control Number: 2022945541

Printed in China

Seahorse Publishing Company
www.seahorsepub.com

Published in the United States
Seahorse Publishing
PO Box 771325
Coral Springs, FL 33077

SEAHORSE PUBLISHING